ALL STAR BLUEGRASS JAM ALONG

Backups, Lead Parts and Note-For-Note Transcriptions
for 21 Essential Tunes

FIDDLE
FEATURING
DAROL ANGER

ISBN-13: 978-1-59773-127-0
ISBN-10: 1-59773-127-7

Box 340 • Woodstock, NY 12498
www.homespun.com

EXCLUSIVELY DISTRIBUTED BY

7777 W. BLUEMOUND RD. P.O. BOX 13819 MILWAUKEE, WI 53213

TABLE OF CONTENTS

INTRODUCTION

This unique series of books was designed to teach aspiring pickers twenty-one of the most widely known songs and instrumentals in the bluegrass repertoire. These are essential tunes for soloists, jammers or members of any bluegrass band. You can be sure that one or more of these will come up in almost every session you are in.

Each book and CD features a different instrument – guitar, banjo, fiddle, mandolin or bass - so that all members of your band can learn their parts. We have employed the services of some of the best-known and most talented pickers in the bluegrass world, experienced professional musicians who want to help you play better on your chosen instrument. Here's the way it works:

On the CD, the backup band (David Grier, Matt Flinner and Todd Phillips) plays the chord changes to each tune several times through at a slow-to-moderate tempo. The lead soloist plays his version of the basic melody, so you can learn it in its most elemental form. The second time he plays it in a slightly more adventurous way, to give you an idea as to where the tune can be taken in an improvised solo.

As the band plays its rhythmic accompaniment, the soloist drops out for several choruses, providing solid backup tracks for a fun and productive practice session.

The book provides you with printed notation and/or tablature so that you can learn to play intros, endings and both of the solos in note-for-note detail. You won't find a better way to learn important tunes and improve your instrumental technique. Once you have mastered these tunes, it will be much easier for you to tackle just about any others that come along.

Every member of your band should have the book that features his or her instrument, so each player can learn the parts. Get together with friends, join a jam session or put it all together with your band, and let it rip.

Have fun!

Bill Cheatham

Intro

A **Theme**

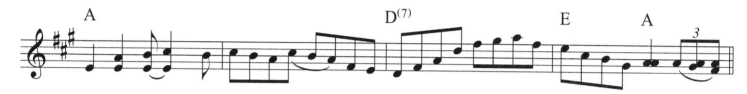

B

Solo

A

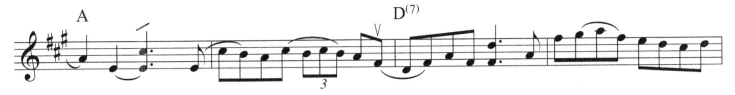

B

Ending

Blackberry Blossom

Theme

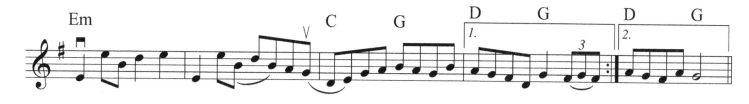

Solo

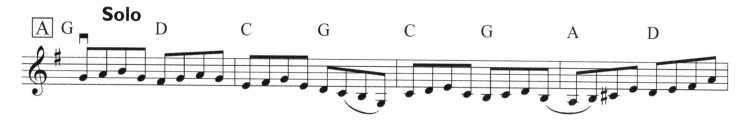

Ending

Black Mountain Rag

A Solo

B

C

Ending

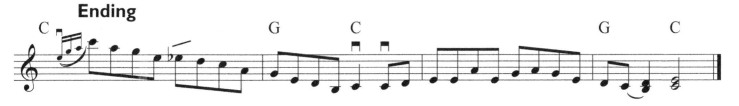

Farewell Blues

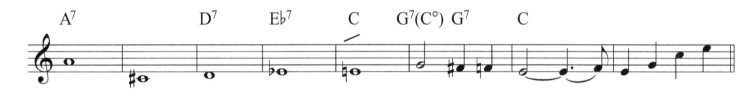

Ending

I'll Fly Away

Theme

(Verse)

(Chorus)

Solo

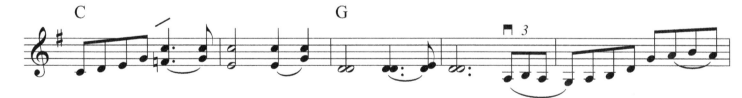

Footprints in the Snow

Theme

(Verse)

(Chorus)

Solo

All the Good Times Are Past and Gone

Theme

Swing tempo

Solo

Solo 2

In the Pines

Theme

Solo

Ending

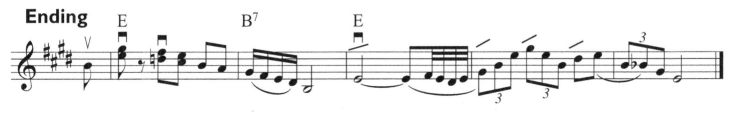

I Am a Pilgrim

Theme

Solo

Ending

John Hardy

3rd Time

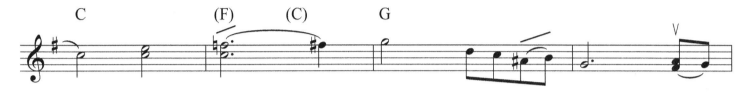

Solo

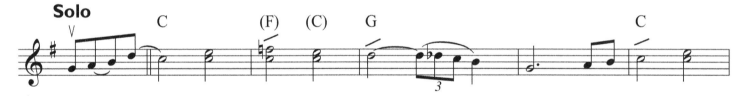

Little Maggie

New River Train

Theme

Solo

2nd Solo

3rd Solo

Ending

Old Joe Clark

Theme

Solo

Solo 2

Pretty Polly

Theme & Variation

Solo

Don't That Road Look Rough and Rocky

Theme

Backup fills

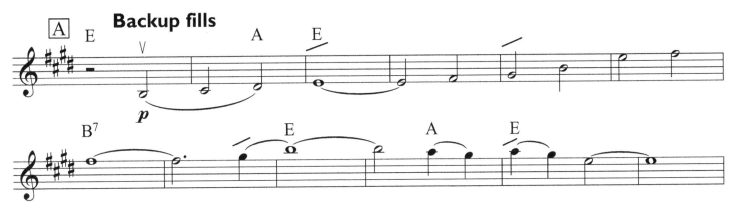

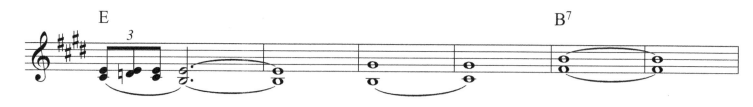

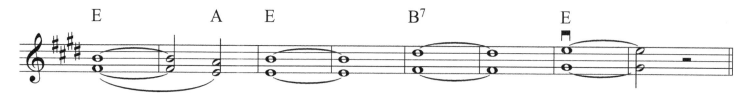

Ending

Sally Ann

Intro

A¹ **Theme**

A²

B

A¹ **Solo**

Solo 2

(Last Time)

Sittin' on Top of the World

Theme

Solo

Backup fills

Solo 2

Soldier's Joy

Theme

Solo

Ending

Roll in My Sweet Baby's Arms

Theme

Solo

Fills

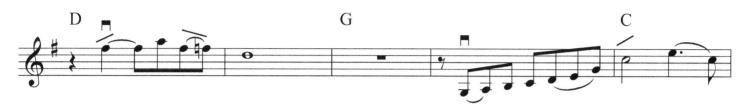

Solo 2

Way Downtown

Theme

Solo

Solo 2

Ending

Down in the Willow Garden

Theme

Solo

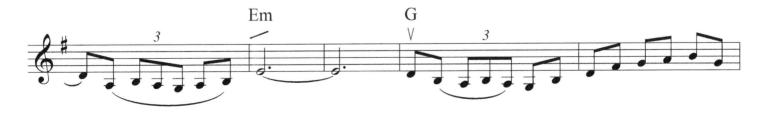

Fills

(Last time)

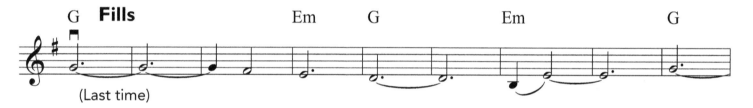

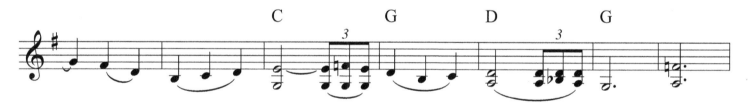

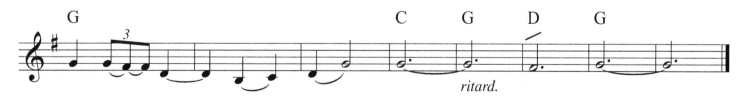

ritard.

Transcription: Tristan Clarridge

Inscription: Tristan Clarridge, John Roberts